OLD REDDITCH

being an early history of the town (1800-1850)

William Avery

THE OLD LOCK-UP - "THE HOLE"

"In 1824, the only really public building in the town with any pretensions to architecture was completed. This was "The Hole"."

Frontispiece

OLD REDDITCH
being an early history of the town (1800-1850)

by William Avery
edited by Anne Bradford

Illustrations by Norman Neasom

Hunt End Books

Hunt End Books
66 Enfield Road, Hunt End, Redditch,
Worcestershire, B97 5NH, England

Published 1999
ISBN 0-9519481 2 1

Cover and book design by John Bradford

Made and printed in Great Britain by
Redwood Books

Front cover: The centre of Redditch. Date unknown but before 1855.
Courtesy Norman Neasom

Acknowledgements

When Ray Taylor went to a local book sale in the summer of 1997, he noticed a tattered booklet with a dark yellow cover, and scribbled across the top was '£10, Rare'. He had found a copy of 'Old Redditch', by William Avery, who was then living in Headless Cross. Ray's sister-in-law, Hilary, found the document so interesting that she passed a copy to Anne Bradford, proprietor of Hunt End Books, who decided to republish. Norman Neasom heard about the project and offered to provide the illustrations.

Thanks are therefore due to Ray and Hilary Taylor, also to Joanne Glover, the needle-making expert at Forge Mill, Philip Davis of Redditch Library and Irene Orlik, for their help and advice.

This is the history of Redditch as William Avery knew it and although every effort has been made to check the text, subsequent research may have proved him wrong on an occasional minor detail.

The wording of the original document has not been changed except for a few typographical corrections, however, some of the paragraphs have been moved so that students can refer more easily to certain topics. Headings have been inserted for the same reason.

Introduction

The contents of this book were first published in 1887 by the *Redditch Indicator*, and were compiled from a series of lectures given by William Avery in Redditch during the winter of 1886.

Despite his evident lack of education he was well-respected in Redditch and during his life-time he held a number of important posts, principally JP for Worcestershire, President of the Liberal Association, Vice-President of the Redditch Building Society and member of the Alcester Board of Guardians. A keen musician, he was chapel organist for 50 years. He took an active part in establishing the Redditch School of Art, then situated at Bates Hill. It is therefore appropriate that the illustrations are provided by the retired head of Redditch School of Art, Norman Neasom.

This is a personal account of the story of Redditch from 1800 to about 1850. The author is said to be William Avery but as he lived from about 1832 to 1899, how did he manage to produce the history of Redditch from 1800 onwards?

As a sideline to working in the needle trade, William Avery made engraved brass needle cases. Some of them have moving parts so that when the needle case is opened, the needles spring into view, each size in its own compartment. They are very much a collector's item, so much so that any brass needle case tends to be known as an 'Avery'. Very little is known about their manufacture, for example, it is not known where in Redditch they were made.

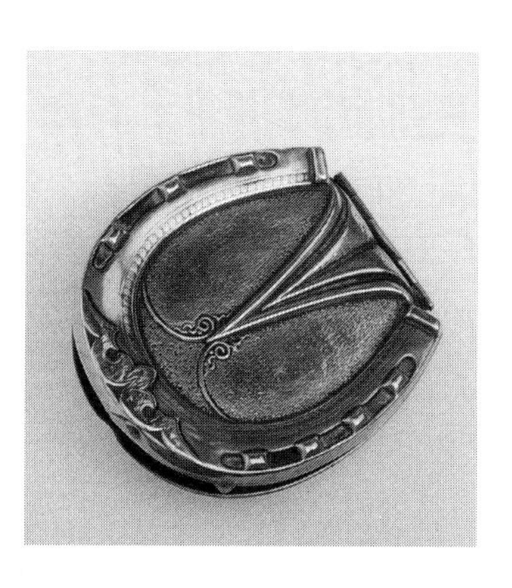

The answer lies in the last paragraph of the book, where he explains that his father began writing the history of Redditch, and he has added to it. It was therefore William Avery's grandfather who is referred to in the first few pages as a penniless inventor and the designer of the Round House.

In the final paragraph, Avery reveals that his father died in the cholera epidemic of 1832. This was probably the year in which Avery was born. The sad fact is, therefore, that William Avery knew little more about his father than we do. It was only from his father's written work that he was aware of his great character, with his enthusiasm for life, his intelligent perception and his wry humour shining through adversity. This book stands as a memorial to the father that he never knew.

The right-hand needle case is in the Forge Museum, the other three are courtesy Alan Foxall.

Redditch and the Needles before William Avery

Next time you pick up a sewing needle, bear in mind that you are using one of man's oldest tools, perhaps going back as far as 26,000 BC! From the time that man first began wearing clothes he required a needle. The first needles were probably nothing more than a splinter of bone sharpened by a stone flint. Instead of an eye, a thin strip of leather or gut was looped over the end of the splinter and secured. Later needles were more like crochet hooks, with a hook at one end to draw the leather through the skins. The earliest needles in the British Museum have holes drilled in the bone, through which sinew or fibre could be threaded. With the discovery of metals came a thinner and stronger needle, bronze needles dating back to 5,000 BC have been found around the Mediterranean and South West Asia. When the Iron Age arrived in about 100 BC, needles were probably made of iron.

Not long after the battle of Hastings in 1066, work began on the Bayeaux tapestry, and anyone who has seen it will know that the craftswomen must have been working with fine quality needles. These could not have come from Redditch, as the town did not then exist. It was not until about 1140 that twelve white-robed monks arrived to found Bordesley Abbey. Redditch began to grow round the Abbey walls, its sole purpose being to serve the Abbey.

There is no written evidence of needle-making until 1370 and that was in Nuremburg, Germany. The Spanish claim that the art of needle-making was learned from them and as they were famous for their swords, this could have been possible. Sometime later, needlemaking could have been taking place at Bordesley Abbey. The monks would have learned the art from the monks of Tintern Abbey who were well-known for their expertise in steel making and wire drawing. The wire would have been brought from Tintern Abbey by boat to Marlcliff (about three-quarters of a mile south of Bidford-on-Avon) then by pack horse or donkey along Ryknield Street to Bordesley Abbey.

In 1540, Henry VIII dissolved the Abbey but wealthy local landowners would have taken the lay brethren into their homes to continue the manufacture of needles. There is no doubt that by the 1800's, each separate family had become experts in one of the many different operations required to make

a needle, so packets of needles would be passed from family to family until the final product was achieved. Needle-making was a cottage industry, eventually stretching from Salford Priors, Inkberrow and Alvechurch to Tanworth-in-Arden, and employing 2,000 men, women and children.

Elizabeth I (1558-1603) persuaded needlemakers from Germany and Holland to settle in London. A Charter was granted to the Needlemakers in 1656 by Oliver Cromwell, the only Charter ever granted by a non-monarch.

BORDESLEY ABBEY

A painting of Bordesley Abbey as envisaged by J M Woodward, 1866. The abbey was founded in 1140 and dissolved by Henry VIII in 1540.

The Guildhall of the Needlemakers was in Threadneedle Street, a corruption of 'three needles' featured on their coat of arms.

Trade restrictions were so severe that in 1650 a breakaway group left London and set up business in Long Crendon, Buckinghamshire. In 1666 The Great Fire of London burned down many London workshops so workers travelled to Long Crendon to join other needlemakers.

Needles have always been a valuable trading commodity; they were essential items which were easily portable and relatively damage-free. Vast areas of Canada and North America changed hands from the Red Indians to the settlers for a dozen or so packets of Redditch needles. In the Sudan in the mid 1800s a packet of needles could buy you a wife!

In the late eighteenth century the industrial revolution arrived. The needlemakers of Long Crendon migrated again, this time to Redditch where the rivers and streams provided better water power. Water mills mushroomed along local rivers and streams, built mostly by wealthy land owners. At first, these were used mainly for scouring and polishing and as the century moved forward more and more processes were moved into the factory. But here we come into the age of William Avery. Let him take up the story.

William Avery 1832-1899
Courtesy Mike Wojczynski

WILLIAM AVERY - HIS LIFE STORY

I was born of poor but respectable parents in the small and unfrequented village of Redditch. Though present at the event, I cannot exactly fix the date, but I may say I came in with the nineteenth century. I was anxious to have noted down the exact date, but on looking over the register I found that when it was removed from the "Old Abbey Chapel" to the "New Chapel on the Green", waste paper was a scarce commodity, and many of the leaves, including that on which my name was inscribed, had been utilised to wrap up "dabs" of hooks sent into the factory. However, I know it was in the year 1800, because it was that year when bread was so dear, and the riots and siege of Redditch, spoken of by the Bromsgrove poet Crane, took place on the 9th of May of that year, when the Bromsgrove Volunteers were brought over to quell the disturbance. I have heard many a time about this visitation, and with what firmness and prudence the volunteers met the violent attack of the rioters, several of whom were apprehended, but discharged on finding sureties for their future good behaviour.

THE SIEGE OF REDDITCH, 1800

The siege of Redditch, I was there all the while,
With nothing to eat but a piece of a tile;
Men, women and children, with trade all alive;
Clods, pebbles, and brickbats sent at us full drive.
Sent at us on purpose to batter our pates;
Tongs, shovels. and pokers, and cheeks of old grates;
A line of stout women, with ladles three deep;
Determined to drive us or send us to sleep.
The leader well armed with a stout wooden crutch
Ten women to one Bromsgrove man, is too much.
The sun sunk away at the sight of the fun,
The moon at the brightest, to light us to run.
When quarrels are up to a terrible pitch,
Be off, like Crane, from the siege of Redditch.
I'm singing of sieges, your chance is but small,
The siege of Redditch is the flogger of all.

THE SIEGE OF REDDITCH

The bread riot of 1800 was a national uprising, brought about by the high price of bread. Until the late eighteenth century, England was able to provide enough grain for its population, but then the home supply was not sufficient and the French wars cut off foreign supplies, with the result that the price of bread soared.
A volunteer police force was hastily assembled at Bromsgrove to quell the Redditch riots but 'ten women to Bromsgrove man is too much' and the volunteers beat a hasty retreat, taking refuge in the Fox and Goose at Tardebigge.

The events of my early life were for many years matters of tradition. I may say, however, that I was "one of a thousand", for I believe I was the unit who led the 999 Redditch sheep out of their hundreds into their thousands, and now see how even the thousands have increased! My father was by trade, or rather profession (for it went but little further than this), a *"soft worker", and on account of his utter disregard of the application necessary to the completion of his work, we found the soft working a very hard way of getting our bread. My father was by no means a man who might be called indolent, for he had always some scheme in his head and some work in his hand; but because his brains worked faster than his fingers he never completed any of the many inventions he commenced, and which would have been of lasting benefit to

**A soft worker is someone who works on the needles before they have been hardened by dipping into oil or water.*

the place and have put us in comfortable circumstances. Round about us were strewn unfinished models of point machines, stamps and presses, hook-bearding and bending tools, and even a machine for sewing, but all wanting some last touch to complete them, and the shop became like a haunted room - haunted with the helpless, nameless ghosts of infants that died at their birth - the ghosts of vain and fruitless projects.

Often when we were pressed for money he would so infuse his spirit into the creditor that he had no heart to press him, believing that in a short time the machine and fortune would be made together.

A NATIONAL LOTTERY

Once when more than usually involved, my father managed to get a share in the National Lottery. Mr. Mence, of the Unicorn, was agent at the time. From that moment his mind was perfectly at ease; the prize would pay all his debts, and leave a handsome sum with which to carry out his ideas. So elated was he that we feared for his reason, but these fears were groundless, for long before his blank was drawn he had almost forgotten the lottery in a new method of hardening needles, which was again in due time abandoned.

THE ROUND HOUSE

Demolished around 1900, it was situated on the east side of Mount Pleasant, between Beaufort Street and the present Council House, directly over the old railway tunnel.

THE ROUND HOUSE

The brothers Sheward, Quakers, (who built the Friends' Meeting House near Messrs. Milwards' factory in 1704) were the first needlemakers in Redditch of whom there is any record. The manufacture of fishhooks was first introduced into Redditch by Walter Brian about 1776.

It was a grand day for my father when he persuaded Mr. Sheward, the needle master (who lived at "The Grove House") to build the "Round House". He was sure that a windmill could be built on the turbine principle, with the sails inside. The mill was constructed, and bade for to be a success, when it had to be abandoned, as my father suddenly turned his attention to a mill to be worked by steam.

WILLIAM AVERY'S SCHOOLDAYS

As soon as I was old enough to be in anyone's way, my scholastic duties began. The first who commenced directing my enquiring mind was Mrs. Biddle, in Evesham Street. When I was about six years old I went for a year to the finishing school kept by Mr. Henry James, in Evesham Street. This was a mixed school, the terms ranging from fourpence to tenpence a week - regulated by the class of studies pursued - with an extra charge in winter time for fire. The style of teaching was one which would not, perhaps, be approved of by the present inspectors of schools, what was learnt was imparted on the stick principle, and was consequently remembered. The school was held in various houses, until about the year 1810 the Earl of Plymouth built an infant school on the site occupied by the School of Art, and now the Local Board.

I may here record the death of Mr. and Mrs. Henry James, for few who lived in the town exercised greater influence over the generation which has almost passed away. Mr. James died, October 19th 1836, aged 77, and his wife followed him, January 20th 1837, aged 76.

The only other academy of importance in the place at this time was in Salter's Yard, conducted by Mr Stephen Wyers. I may here mention that the "Free School" was not opened until February 21st, 1820.

REDDITCH - THE TOWN

It may not be uninteresting to some to know something about what Redditch was like when I was a lad. Most of the houses were to be found on the Green, and these can easily be noted. First of all, then, the Green was mounded round, and a few trees stood on it. Mr Waring, among other occupations, let out horses for hire, and these were fastened in this enclosure. In time, the fences were allowed to fall away, and gravel pits and sand holes took their places. Mr. Waring lived where Mr Brunton lived (now Mr Charles White). Where the new bank now stands, Masters had a blacksmith's shop. His son was a favourite amongst us lads, because he generally made the Guys for the 5th of November. Izods and Allens lived about the same place. Near Mr Smith, the surgeon's, there was a wheelwright's and blacksmith's shop, and on the opposite side "Berrod" Clarke, baker, and Carr, butcher, lived. Then came the Fox and Goose, kept by Samuel Fowkes, "a good neighbour and friend to the poor". Near the "Luton House" John George, the head grocer, sanded his sugar; a large elm tree grew on this spot and continued to be an ornament to the village until it was "improved" off the land on the 13th March 1820 to make room for bricks and mortar. Under it lived Mr. Taylor, surgeon, and next Gruby, the biggest man in the town, kept a grocer's shop. Bray kept a public house where Mr. Smith now lives; and then we come to the corner where one of the most noted Redditch characters resided - Timothy Munslow. He manufactured cakes and mutton pies which he carried round on Saturday nights to the public houses for sale, and warmed them up every subsequent Saturday till they were disposed of. Of this business he enjoyed a monopoly, but what endeared him most to our young hearts was the fact that he possessed a troupe of fiery steeds - that is, they would have been fiery had they been burnt, for they were made of wood. Our Redditch poet (Hollis) of that time thus immortalizes him and his chargers:-

"Old Timothy Mousetrap and his wooden team,
To get children's peace he had got a good scheme."

At the opposite corner, where Mrs. Palmer (now Mr Cranmore) lives, stood the smithy of Benjamin Perry and Sons, the principal blacksmiths, and makers and menders of the soft-workers' tools. Some small houses stood between this and the Unicorn, which was then kept by Mr. Mence.

WAN
FO
1996
N. NEASOM
r e h W

TIM MUNSLOW

A notable Redditch character in the 18th century. He made cakes and mutton pies which he sold in the local pubs on Saturday nights and each subsequent Saturday night until they were disposed of. He also kept wooden horses at the fair.
His son was reputed to have shod the Duke of Wellington's horse at the battle of Waterloo. His house stood at the corner of old Evesham Street and market place.

Where Mr. Monks' house now stands, Morris, the grocer and carpenter, lived. Then, the house which lies back, hiding its face with ivy, was kept by Scambler, the baker. We used to give two shillings for a loaf of bread then; we took it with thankfulness and asked no questions as to whether it was "fancy bread" or not. Where the Birmingham bank now stands, Lawyer Gardner kept chambers. Reading, the grocer, lived as his next neighbour. Where Mr. Jeffries lives, John Gittens carried on his building trade. There were a few small houses near the Crown; Wapping was in existence and "Little Wapping" was springing up. "Newend" was older than either of these and all were inhabited by soft-workers.

The public institutions were the stocks and whipping post, situate opposite the Fox and Goose, and the Volunteers, who used to parade twice a week on the Green, under the command of Captain Mence of the Unicorn; Lieutenant Kendrick, the butcher; and Ensign Mucklow, who was a farmer down Beoley Lane.

THE OLD LOCK-UP - "THE HOLE"

I well remember that under the infant school (built in 1810) a sort of cellar was made to serve the purposes of a public prison, open to all without distinction of creed or sex.

In 1824, the only really public building in the town with any pretensions to architecture was completed. This was *"The Hole". The want of such an institution had, I suppose, long been felt, for a number of needle manufacturers met at the Fox and Goose and subscribed a considerable sum toward the building of this little Bastille. As its days are now numbered, I may say that the style of its architecture was the same as that of the new Houses of Parliament at Westminster, and its ventilation and lighting very little better. The first person who took up his abode in its castellated walls was for hare-catching. The upper room of the "Old Lock-up" as it is now called, was, I believe, intended for the dwelling of the constable, Salter Allday. However, it was occupied by an eccentric character, Lawyer Guardner, a relic of one of the old families of Redditch.

In 1825, another building with a more pretentious name, but with less stability, was erected in Beoley Lane. It rejoiced in the name of "The Castle". Its walls were one brick thick, set up edgeways, and as there was, from its construction, a chance of not only living in it, but dying in it also, only one person was found with courage enough to occupy it. Afterwards, it served as

* *See frontispiece*

a place of amusement for Redditch boys, who used to show their daring by running up and down the stairs. It was taken down about the year 1840, when a ladder which was used in its erection and had never been removed, served the workmen to pull it down.

OFF TO WORK

But to return for a time to myself. I was taken away from school just when I began to learn, for we must all work, and I was introduced into my father's trade. The shop was in the back room of the house and was filled with windows, which seemed like eyes, through which the room was staring with all its might to see where the next meal was to come from.

DRAWING THE WIRE

In order to get the wire to the correct thickness, it was first drawn through a series of holes made in a piece of hard steel.

Most of the work was done away from the factories and was fetched by us a packet at a time, in points, cut through. The wire was all made from common steel (for the best cast steel was not then invented) and gave great trouble in working up; for where there was a flaw the wire split up when the needle was made. The points were first cut through and the top part flattened. Then a punch was used for "first eyeing", which was merely making the impression of the eye, the wire being laid during this process on a piece of lead. The second operation consisted of another and sharper punch, which fitted the square indentation, being driven through to form the eye. This was repeated from the other side. The "gutters" were next made with a jagged saw-like knife in the form of a cleaver. When this was done, the head was filed round, and the needle was made. They then went through the process of straightening, which was merely rolling them on a stone with a bent iron bar till then had rolled themselves out straight.

A man and his wife could make about 5,000 a day for which about 5s was paid, but as soon as the children were about eight or nine years of age they were brought into the shops, where they worked at the "cammou", so that a man having a quiver full of youngster was happy indeed. No Factory Inspectors or Acts had been invented, and the foundation of many a sickly constitution was laid, for many of the "soft-workers" liked their beer, as well as their children, and what were children intended for if not to work!

NEEDLE POINTING - 'BORN TO DIE YOUNG'

The effects of pointing were clearly visible on the workmen, and with hard drinking, hard fighting, and when so disposed, hard working, their constitutions soon began to give way.

The following line by E. Elliot graphically describes the condition of the pointer at this time:-

There draws the grinder his laborious breath.
There, coughing at his deadly trade he bends,
Born to die young, he fears no man, nor death,
Scorning the future, what he earns he spends.
Yet Abraham and Elliot both in vain
Bid science on his cheek prolong the bloom;
He would not live! He seems in haste to gain
The undisturbed asylum of the tomb,
And, old at two-and-thirty, meets his doom.

NEEDLE POINTING

After being drawn to the correct thickness, the wire was cut into pieces the length of two needles and pointed at each end on a grindstone by the grinders or needle-pointers. After pointing, two needle eyes were formed in the middle of these wire pieces using a kick stamp and a fly press.

On the 11th January, 1822, Mr. J. H. Abraham came from Sheffield with a newly-invented muzzle of magnets, which was to take away all the steel from the dust the pointers inhaled, and so prevent the *"rot". Though there was no doubt of their being a preventative to a certain extent, they shared the fate of the magnets afterwards used behind the stones, i.e., broken up, as it was feared that if the danger and unhealthiness were taken away, too many would be induced by the high rate of wages to learn their trade, and consequently cause a fall in prices.

The effects of needle-pointing were well shown in the following statement drawn up by Mr. Osborne many years ago:- "To show the injurious effects of this branch of the trade upon the human frame the following startling facts may be mentioned:- About a year ago (1839) the manufacturers proposed to establish a benefit society for the pointers, and with this view the name and

"The rot" is the lung pneumoconiosis, caused by inhaling certain dust particles.

age of each one, and the number of years he had worked at needle-pointing, was obtained. There were 150 names on the list: the average age was under twenty-eight and the time employed at pointing under eight years". But now these men, formerly so thoughtless and careless of their lives, are so particular that they will only work at those mills where the pointers' "life preserver" - the fan - is used: and this is perhaps one of the best proofs of the advancement that has taken place amongst the artizans of our town.

TROUBLE AT THE MILL

The summer of 1826 was one of the hottest and driest ever remembered; the crops of hay were not more than one-eighth of their usual quantity, and the corn was almost all housed by Redditch Fair. Mr. Walter Walford, indeed, built a wheat rick as early as July 20th.

At this time the pointers were on strike for an increase of wages, and on July 26th, 1826, twenty-six of them came to Beoley Mill on their way to Studley. The principal promoters of the strike were Thomas Merry, Bonny Southall, Crem Fisher, Uncle Hill and Charles Hughes. They held their meetings in a bye lane between Green Lane and Crabbs Cross. Every meeting was well supplied with bread and cheese and ale, and continued as long as the weather and provisions held out. The subject of the strike was to resist a reduction of sixpence per day, and lasted three weeks, when the masters gave in and they returned to work.

THE MOST SERIOUS STRIKE EVER KNOWN

In 1830 the pointers struck a second time. On this occasion it was against the masters deducting threepence a packet for "cutting back". It lasted a few days only, when the masters gave way. A third strike in 1844 was successfully carried out against Mr. John Chambers for introducing a pointing machine. The machine was broken up and the people went to work again. The pointers formed themselves into a union, and in 1846 the most serious strike ever known in the trade took place. It lasted for many months, and great distress prevailed. The masters took upon themselves the task of regulating the prices for pointing; lowering them where they were over-charged and increasing them where too low. The masters acted with as great an unanimity as the men. After one of their meetings the masters issued the following circular, to which was annexed their revised list of prices:-

"At a meeting of the needle manufacturers resident in Redditch, Worcestershire, and its vicinity, held at the offices of Mr. Edward Browning, Solicitor, Redditch, the 9th day of September 1846, in consequence of the Needle Pointers, notwithstanding their present high wages, having again demanded an exorbitant advance thereof, William Hemming, Esq., in the chair, it was resolved unanimously that the following list of prices now prefixed and agreed upon, be hereafter paid by the manufacturers for pointing the descriptions of needles and fish-hooks stated in such lists; and the several manufacturers whose names are hereunderwritten mutually agree to and with each other not to pay any greater or other prices than those stated in the said list. That these resolutions be printed, and distributed in Redditch, Feckenham, Studley, Alcester and its vicinity."

(Signed) William Hemming, Chairman."

This was signed by fifty-four manufacturers, the larger proportion of whom are now dead.

The strike was continued - though in good spirit, no violence or unfriendly-feeling being exhibited on either side - until the 16th November 1846, when the pointers accepted the masters' terms, broke up their union, and commenced work again.

STAMPS, DIES AND RIOTS!

About 1828-9, preparations were being made which would entirely alter the circumstances of the town. The "soft-workers", work as hard as they might, could only produce a very limited quantity of needles, and for some years past - perhaps as far back as 1790 - John Farr, who had retired to Alcester, commenced making the large needles, such as sail and pack needles, by means of a stamp and dies. In 1800, an attempt was made at Washford Mill to make as many as a hundred needles at a time: but they succeeded in making thirty-five only, and the thing dropped through, on account of the person who constructed the machine disappearing from the place. Still, there were many with the idea of stamping in their minds. Amongst others, Brandon Whittle, who we must look upon as the first stamper, though the stamp as we have it now was perhaps first suggested by Farr (of Coughton), John Crook (of Studley), who made "long eyes" and quilting, and Cook (of Hadenway), who made bodkins. Among the early users of stamps, I may mention Mr.

Abel Morrall (of Green Lane), and Mr T. Baylis (of Bredon). The first needles stamped were very roughly made, with square eyes, to imitate as much as possible those made by hand. So very rough and crude were they, that they went by the not very euphonious title of "eyes and limbs".

It seems singular that, though Redditch has been the centre of needle manufacture and most of the improvements in the processes have been made in the neighbourhood, it was not until the autumn of 1830 that stamps were first used in the town. As soon as this was done, the "soft workers" began to express murmurs of discontent, and loud expressions of dissatisfaction was uttered, until at length they determined to take action. One Monday morning posters were circulated calling on the workmen to meet near "The Big Pool" to determine what should be done, it being understood that hammers might be wanted. A large number of working men assembled, and on December 2nd, 1830, a deputation went to meet the masters, who were assembled at the Unicorn, to consider what was to be done, and to arrange about prices. (I may mention that a week previous the bell of the old chapel had been rung to call the respectable inhabitants together, and the Earl of Plymouth came over from Hewell for the purpose of swearing them in as special constables.).

While the deputation attended at the Unicorn, the meeting at "The Big Pool" was addressed by Jason Boulton, "Lawyer" Court, and others, and becoming impatient for action, Dunsby was ordered to get out his fife, and Seth Boulton his drum. Led by this "band" the men proceeded down to Bredon and smashed up all Mr. T. Baylis's stamps. They then determined to go on to Studley and neighbourhood and finish their work of destruction. Mr. A. Morrall got his stamps out and hid them in the pool near his house, but before the mob reached there they met a man or "a ghost" and fearing resistance the riot suddenly collapsed.

Several of the principal rioters were brought before the magistrates; six were convicted at the Worcester Assizes, 1831, and from that time stamps became generally used. I have heard that these riots were the cause of the Hewell Yeomanry being formed. Many of the tenantry were formed into squad of mounted constables, and were then continued as they now exist.

DRILLING AND A PEEPING TOM

Some time previous to this (1830), William Green, of Astwood Bank, invented drilling the eyes of needles. This he kept a profound secret, and obtained a price ranged from 3s to 4s6d a thousand. The needles were *drilled

** Drilled in the soft ie excess metal is removed before the needles have been hardened*

in the soft, and the most extraordinary thing was that they were continued to be stamped square-eyed. It was not until sometime after that the eyes were made round. When Green was working one night some curious person managed to place a ladder against his window, and seeing how the operation of drilling was performed, commenced on his account, and others sprang up, until the system was universally adopted.

When drilling in the bright was first done, the needles were blued by sticking about a dozen in a cork and then holding the eyes in the flame of a candle. These were then drilled once and counter-sunk twice. Oval-eyed needles were first made about the year 1839, and then the drill had to share with the burnishing machine the work of making the eye a safe place for the thread.

UNWELCOME IMPROVEMENTS

Redditch can supply many instances showing the obstacles which have been thrown in the way of improvements. I remember when we met the masters in the Lion Room about the soft-work business, Mr. T. Turner said he was the first who introduced drilling into the town, and up rose one of the oldest manufacturers of the town and pettishly exclaimed, "Then you are the person who has brought upon the town the greatest curse that it could be visited with". Time has shown, however, that man may be in error even with regard to improvements.

TYING THE SETT

The needles were neatly layered with a mixture of powdered stone and soft soap on a strip of canvas which was then rolled into a sausage (the sett) and tied tightly with strong twine. The sett was then ready to go under the scouring bed for polishing. Each sett could hold up to 60,0000 needles and weighed about 13 kilos (28 lbs).

NEEDLE POLISHING

The 'setts' were put under the scouring bed runners and rolled backwards and forwards nby the powerful machinery of the water mill for eight to ten hours. The needles were then taken out and washed in the special tray shown on the left of the drawing. They were tied up in another sett and this time layered with a mixture of putty powder and olive oil to achieve a glaze. They went back in the scouring beds for six to eight hours, were taken out and washed again, then dried by rolling in barrels of sawdust. Special fanning out trays (as shown on the left) separated the needles from the sawdust.

IMPROVEMENT IN HARDENING PROCESSES

At the latter part of 1839, and the beginning of 1840, an improvement in hardening caused great excitement in Redditch. Mr. Joseph Turner had been over to Hatherage where he saw that a certain mode of hardening improved the second quality steel. When he returned he began to experimentalize on needles, and soon found that using oil instead of water in hardening kept the needles straighter. People thought that a very important branch of the trade would be ruined and about 700 women thrown out of employment. A committee was formed and subscriptions raised to buy up the hardeners at the factories where the new process was used. Some of the hardeners were not objectors to the system, and when the money failed to keep the men out they went in again. A public meeting was held in the *Rifle Corps Room on

The Rifle Corps Room has now been demolished but stood in the area behind Smallwood Hospital.

10th February 1840 (the day the Queen married) when all the masters and a great crowd of people assembled. The meeting was a warm one. The people first demanded and then craved that the masters should give up the oil hardening, on the grounds that "if the employment was taken away from the women they would be compelled to take to a life of prostitution". (It has always seemed to be a great mistaken notion in Redditch that women were ordained to work in a factory instead of attending to their home duties).

At last, there was a sort of understanding that the new system would be discontinued, though, as Mr. Hemming said, "It is of no use your supposing that if this is an improvement it will be given up; the interests of the trade will not allow it". The Messrs. Turner continued their hardening, and Mr. J. Turner, who lived in Bredon, was mobbed, and his hardener, Thomas Dolphin, was burnt in effigy. Leaders were found to stimulate this feeling, and after enduring this kind of persecution for about two months, Mr. Turner, with his family and workpeople, removed to Stratford-on-Avon, where for some time he continued his trade. It is needless to remark that the new system of hardening was quickly adopted by all the manufacturers, and that at the present time it would be a difficult thing to induce straighteners to work at needles hardened in water.

SECRET IMPROVEMENTS IN POLISHING

In the early part of 1829, a new method of finishing needles was invented by Mr. Abner Melen. Up to this time needles were polished on a blue stone rubbed over with charcoal, and much time and great care were required to prevent the needles becoming "magnified", on account of the hardness of the tool. Mr Melen's invention was a very simple one, and consisted in covering a spindle with leather and dressing it with a paste consisting of emery powder and glue. He succeeded in keeping it secret for a number of years, but at length the buffs were discovered, and now the finishers generally dress their own.

MONEY OR MOUSETRAPS?

The only other matter of importance in the trade of the town that I shall speak about is the *"Truck" agitation of 1848. Very bitter and angry feelings were engendered by the system, which was carried on to such an extent by

**The truck system is one in which the workmen are paid for their services in kind not cash. It was made illegal in 1831.*

some that when a man went up to settle he did not know whether he would be paid in money or mousetraps. The system, however, in its more public form was put a stop to; but another, that of "shop-rent", took its place. When a person has a fair week's work it simply becomes a mere matter of price for labour, but where a whole week's rent is deducted from one or two days' labour it is discreditable to the employer and oppressive to the work people.

NEEDLEWORKERS IN FRANCE

At the latter end of 1849, the quiet of the poor Rifle Corps Room was again disturbed by a great meeting. This time it was to consider the advent of a Frenchman who had come over for the purpose of inducing some of the Redditch hands to return with him to superintend some needle works in France. Of course, this public meeting had about the same effect as all the others - none at all. Some persons were induced to go abroad, but most of them soon returned, and very shortly there was not an Englishman working in the French needle factories.

SPECIAL CONSTABLES

I may mention here that there were a great number of incendiary fires in the neighbourhood, on account of the farmers using threshing machines. Some persisted in using them, others gave way; but, to preserve the peace and safety, it was considered necessary to have special protection, and on December 8th 1830, nearly the whole of the working men of Beoley parish went to Brianstones Cross to be sworn in as special constables.

SAINT STEPHEN'S CHAPEL

Passing over the history of Bordesley Abbey from its foundation in 1149 to its dissolution by Henry VIII in 1539, we come to the fact that in 1687 the chapel of Saint Stephen, which stood in the ruins of the Abbey, was endowed with an estate and benefaction, and used by the townspeople as a place of worship until 1807, and the adjoining burial ground was used as a place of interment until about 1805. Those who died from cholera in the epidemic of 1832 were also buried here. In 1713, soon after the chapel had been restored by Nathanial Mugg, Barber's Farm was devised to the vicars of Tardebigge for ever, on condition that they caused preaching to be made once a Sunday at Redditch Chapel, and at the usual times in Tardebigge Church. On May the 1st, the same year, John Allen, Jun. devised a *copyhold messuage or tenement, and lands, meadows, closes, and pastures, in trust to John Field and George Bolton to procure "some sober and good clergyman" to reside at Redditch, and preach a sermon every Sabbath in the chapel of Redditch; and he also devised a further sum of £5 for the encouragement of the said clergyman.

The Gate House Chapel at the ruined Bordesley Abbey, some 3/4 of a mile from the town centre and the place of worship for the people of Redditch

SAINT STEPHENS BECOMES THE CHAPEL ON THE GREEN

In the year 1806, therefore, no place of worship existed in the town. There had been a meeting house of Friends for more than a hundred years, but long before this time it had become unused and now the only place of religious worship was the old Abbey Chapel, which was a Chapel of Ease to Tardebigge. The officiating minister was the Rev. Mr. Richards, who was supposed to have fifty-two sermons, which he regularly read each afternoon during each year he ministered. No-one grumbled at them, for were not the sermons better than the **stipend? In the course of time the discourses became pretty well known, some were liked and others not, so the congregations were regulated by the favour in which the respective sermons were held.

We used to march in order from Mr. James' Sunday School down the Front Hill till we reached the bottom, when discipline was lessened, and we wandered every way but churchwards.

The chapel was the only remnant of the Old Abbey for which little was known, excepting that treasures were found beneath some stone, and that "the place was haunted". It has always been a matter of regret to me that the penny-wise and pound-foolish feeling existed, and that the only visible part of the splendid Abbey of Bordesley, in which "the oldest inhabitants" had worshipped for generations, should be pulled down and drawn up to the Green, to take a very humble position in the old three-windows locomotive-

**Copyhold is a method of holding land, and a messuage is a dwelling house with outbuildings and land.*

*** A stipend is the official income of a member of the clergy.*

looking building which rejoiced in the title of "The Chapel on the Green". Had this piece of vandalism not been committed, we might now be looking upon a remnant of the building erected by Queen Maud, seven or eight centuries back, and musing on the monkish life led.

Mr Clayton was not a member of the "church penitent" but of the "church militant", as was testified by his "punching a fellow's head" in the street on the west side of the chapel yard.

The present building was completed, and on Sunday, April 5th, 1807, it was preached in for the first time by the Rev. R. Cotham of Bromsgrove, who took his text from the 8th chapter of the First Kings and 27th verse, "But will God indeed dwell on the earth? Behold the heaven and heaven of heavens cannot contain thee: how much less this house that I have builded". The chapel was licensed for service, and was not consecrated until the following year, when the Bishop of Chester performed the ceremony on Easter Thursday, April 21st 1809, and preached from 21st chapter of Matthew, 13th verse. Mr. Tordiff was the first curate appointed to the living. He lived with old Mrs. Reading and preached his first sermon on the afternoon of April 5th, 1807. He was followed by the Rev. M. Booker, who was succeeded by Mr. Scott (the son of the commentator) in 1814. After him came Mr. Potts in 1816, Mr. Lee in 1819 and Mr. Clayton in 1820. By the way, it would seem that Mr. Clayton was not a member of the "church penitent" but of the "church militant" as was testified by his "punching a fellow's head" in the street on the west side of the chapel yard. The Rev. G. F. Fessey succeeded, and preached his first sermon on Christmas Day, 1841. The first marriage in the chapel was between Henry Bartleet, widower, and Sarah Bate, widow, September 19th 1808; and the first funeral in the chapel yard was that of an infant son of William and Catherine Smith.

AN ORGAN ARRIVES

For a considerable time the musical part of the service was performed by an excellent choir, which was long celebrated throughout the neighbourhood. In the choir were several fine voices, and these were supported by John Cooper who played the bass viola, James Lee who played the fiddle, and others. The organ was not used until Mid Lent Sunday, March 20th 1814. Mrs. Inman played for the first time on August 24th 1828 and George Sutton, who had built a double bass and played in it in the chapel since August 4th 1822, commenced his duties as organist, August 29th 1830.

The chapel was enlarged in 1817, and after having been painted and decorated, was preached in again on October 21st 1822. A brick wall was built round the yard, which was enlarged and trees planted, after which it was consecrated by the Bishop, December 29th 1827, and the new gallery on the north side was first used on December 16th of the same year. The first confirmation in Redditch was on Thursday, June 13th 1833, and the gallery on the south side of the chapel was first used November 15th 1835. The Royal coat of arms which now adorns the magistrates' room, was placed in the chapel on October 23rd 1836 at a cost of £5. Evening service was commenced by Mr Clayton, May 30th, 1840.

METHODISM ESTABLISHED WITH THE AID OF A CARVING KNIFE

The introduction and progress of Wesleyan Methodism in Redditch might take up many of my pages, but suffice it to say that at the time I was born, Mr. T. Cocker, of Hathersage used to come over *travelling in wire. He saw the gross ignorance and wickedness in which the people lived and, as he passed through Birmingham on his way home, called on the Rev. R. Reece, who was then stationed there, and left a sovereign with him to commence a fund to meet the expenses of preachers from Birmingham to Redditch. In 1807 the

ie he was a representative of a wire company supplying the raw material.

first preacher came over and commenced to preach in the house Mrs. J. Turner, of Bredon. The usual persecution was shown. The people stuck up for their fifty-two sermons, and wanted no more. Their knowledge was already more than their practice, and they were determined to drive away the Methodists. Sunday after Sunday the services in the house were interfered with by the mob who congregated in the neighbourhood, and one night it was determined to cut the work short by a special service. That evening the preacher whom, as usual, came over from Birmingham, had scarcely commenced his service when music was heard advancing. A fifer from a Volunteer Corps, whose name I will not immortalise by mentioning, and a drunken drummer from a village band, with the usual accompaniments of tin kettles and warming pans led on the pious inhabitants of the town, who joined with great heartiness and accord in the music led by the instruments named. The service without very seriously entered the service within, and what was to be done? Mrs Turner, a woman of strong will and heart, was determined to put a stop to the annoyance, or, as young people now-a-days say, "perish in the attempt". She accordingly armed herself with a candle and carving knife, marched into the crowd, pushed on up to the band, and with eyes sparkling with intense feeling, plunged her knife up to the very hilt into - the drum! The persecutors scattered and from that memorable time to the present, I believe, the Methodists have been unmolested and have spread their usefulness over all the needle district.

TROUBLE WITH THE WESLEYANS

In 1832, considerable excitement was caused amongst the Wesleyans in the town by the superintendent of the circuit (the Rev. Mr. Graham) not being willing to allow Miss Butler and other young women to preach. Mr. Breeden, of Derby, who had formerly resided at Redditch, was appealed to, and came over and founded a new society, who called themselves the *Arminians. The Rifle Corps Room was licensed for preaching, and services commenced on the 13th May, 1832. A regular minister was at once appointed - Mr. Slack - who preached for the first time on the following Sunday, May 20th. The society progressed so satisfactorily that a chapel (much smaller than the present one but on the same site) was built, and preached in on the 30th June, 1833.

**Arminianism was a doctrine of man's free will and salvation by faith taught by Jacobus Arminius (1560-1609).*

CHARITY SERMONS

At this time it was the custom for Redditch singers to go to neighbouring churches and give them "a turn" at their charity sermons. On November 18th, 1825, old Mr Cormauls preached three sermons at Tanworth, and the Redditch Choir went thither on Humphries' coach. Large posters had been circulated round the parish, stating that selections from "The Messiah" would be given. And when the Redditch choir arrived at Tanworth, a host of villagers assembled, looking at everything they could see, until at length the double-bass, which had been built by George Sutton and taken over to assist, was taken out of the vehicle. All stood in wonder and awe, none knowing what it was, till one, who had enjoyed peculiar educational advantages, exclaimed to his companions, "I say, that there's the Messiah".

On the night of Tuesday, November 26th, 1826, while Mr Nicklin, the Wesleyan minister, was preaching, some thieves broke into Mr Turner's house, where he lodged, and amongst other things stole a large chest belonging to the minister, and before leaving wrote on the table "Watch and pray". About this time, too, the "Rippling Boys" carried on an extensive system of plundering. The factories were robbed, live animals taken from the fields, and pigs from the sty. However, as many were caught, and the judges were pretty liberal with their sentences, peace and safety at length returned to the neighbourhood after terror and alarm had existed for a considerable period.

DROWNINGS AT BEOLEY BROOK

The roads round about Redditch were of the worst possible description, the best of them being almost impassable, and some of them dangerous. One of the most fatal places in the neighbourhood was the road through Beoley Brook. In my time I can remember several serious accidents, and before then no-one can tell the number of disasters which occurred. Though it is not expressly stated, yet I believe that there the *Rev. John Wesley had a very narrow escape. On his way from Wednesbury to Evesham, accompanied by Messrs. Walsh and Bruce, in August 1756, it states that near Redditch they came to a place which was flooded, and Mr. Bruce, "seeing a footbridge, walked over, leading his horse by a long rein through the water. In an instant the horse disappeared. However, he soon emerged and gained the bank". Mr Wesley gaining experience from this found a safer place farther down

**The Rev. John Wesley (1703-1791) was the founder of the Methodist Church.*

LOADING A CART

'The roads round about Redditch were of the worst possible description, the best of them being almost impassable, and some of them dangerous'.

where he crossed. I do not know of any other place between here and Evesham where this incident could have occurred.

On Saturday, November 10th, 1810, five horses belonging to the Birmingham Brewery were drowned there, and a great number of us boys went down next morning to see them fished out. The carrier, Heath, tried to get through the same place on the 25th January, 1820, when the water was high, and he had a horse drowned. A few days before this he had another and more serious accident befall his family. His son had been out to bring home a load of flour, and crossing over a bridge it broke with the weight of the waggon. The youth was thrown under the load and drowned.

Mr Joseph Turner was driving his sister to Birmingham in a gig on the 28th April, 1825, when by some means as they were passing through the brook the horse got into Hemming's Hole and was drowned. Doubtless other accidents could be enumerated to fill up the dates to 1861, when Henry Garfield lost his life here.

I recount these facts so that they may have some weight with those persons who are now taking into consideration the desirability of arching over the brook and making a safe and permanent road. There is no doubt that the place is dangerous, and should human life be further lost there will be a grave question as to whose door the blame will lie at.

The principal road to Birmingham went this way and along the ancient Rycknield (Icknield) Street, a considerable portion of the road being scarcely wide enough for one vehicle. Formerly bells were fastened to the horses' harness, so that they might by heard by drivers of other vehicles, who were able to wait in some opening and allow the approaching vehicle to pass. Another road to Birmingham went in at the British Needle Mills and round by the Abbey Meadows, but in the years 1825, 1826, 1827, the "Great South Road" was made, which ought to have been carried to Pershore, but which only ran from Birmingham to Blind Lane and back.

TWO NEWSPAPERS BUT ONLY ONE COPY

At this time only one paper was taken in the town, The Courier, and one Birmingham paper, *The Chronicle*. These, Mr. Bartlett used to bring into the "Back Room" or front parlour of the Crown, and with the aid of his silver spectacles, read to those who met regularly to hear the news. I may say here that the few newspapers brought into the town caused a great lack of paper for the general wrapping-up purposes of a household, and an important, and what might have been a serious matter, to one of our townsmen was the consequence. Not so many years since he was engaged in a Chancery suit, and was required to produce the register of his birth. He sought in vain for it and had to get the certificates from the doctor and the nurse who were present when he was born. These he obtained from them when they were on their death beds; and after some time discovered that he was one of the last who had been christened in the Old Abbey Chapel, and the then clerk, who was a fish-hook maker, had, owing to the scarcity of paper, used leaves from the register to wrap up "dabs" of hooks for the factory, as was the case in my instance previously alluded to.

REDDITCH AND THE BATTLE OF TRAFALGAR

By the way, paper making appears to have been an ancient industry in the neighbourhood, for in an account of a perambulation of the bounds of the chapel of Bordesley, in 1600, mention is made of "The New Paper Mill, Little Meadow Corner".

In 1785 Joseph E Webb, of Beoley, bound himself apprentice to James Holyoake, of Tardebigge parish, to learn the art of paper making. The indenture, which bears the signature of Elizabeth and R.H. Guardner as witnesses, is dated 3rd September, 25th year of the reign of George III, 1785. He afterwards worked for Matthew Mills, at the Beoley Paper Mill. His life was not, however, always spent among the sylvan scenes of Beoley, for we learn that afterwards he was valet to Admiral Lord Nelson, and was on board the Victory at the memorable battle of Trafalgar.

REDDITCH AND THE CIVIL WAR

The district appears to have participated to a considerable extent in the troubles and events incidental in the civil war, for we read that in May, 1643, Charles I reviewed 10,000 men at Crabbe Crosse, and in December of the same year, Beoley Hall was burnt by the Parliamentary "souldiers"; goods and cattle plundered and the court rolls destroyed.

REDDITCH AND THE BATTLE OF WATERLOO

I may say in passing that in 1807 there was great excitement about the militia, and many who were drawn provided substitutes at a cost varying from £20 to £40. A sort of benefit society was formed into which certain weekly payments were made, and when any of its members were unfortunately "drawed for the militia" money was provided to employ a substitute.

In 1815 the battle of Waterloo was fought, and Redditch supplied its quota. Amongst those who were there were Avery, Steel of Headless Cross, who was wounded early in the fight, and Tom Wright, who was killed. Jackey Watts had the good fortune, as soon as the battle began, to find a wounded colonel, whom he shouldered, and went so far to the rear that he had not time to return before the fight was ended. Young Timothy Munslow shod the Duke's horse before he entered into the battle. James Baylis was ordered out, but his regiment did not arrive until after the fight was over.

ASHLEIGH WORKS

The factory was a needle mill and is still standing near the centre of Redditch, on the Bromsgrove Road and on the corner of Britten Street.

A MIRACLE PLAY WITH EXTRA COURAGE

The month of June, 1815, will be long remembered by those who were boys at the time. In this month there were great rejoicings through the country on account of the treaty of peace having been signed. The great heart of Redditch throbbed throughout its little body, which burst out into an intense perspiration of feasting and jollity. Never before, nor since, was there seen such fun, but I content myself with relating one instance as a specimen. It was thought the proper thing to revive the old "Miracle Play" system and the subject chosen was "Napoleon imprisoned at Elba". A young apprentice of the town (who afterwards became one of our most respectable manufacturers) having had his face blackened, was dressed as Napoleon. He was then seated on a cask, and escorted by two mounted "Cossacks", with huge lances in their hands. These were accompanied by the multitude to the coal-hole prison under the Infant School, which was Elba in metaphor. For this brilliant exploit, the Cossacks had so inflamed their courage with beer that they began, regardless of nationality or other just cause, to use their weapons on the crowd, who were forced to set on and disarm, them, and secure them in safe keeping until they had slept off the exuberant patriotism.

My father had been for some time preparing a new light, and this evening it was to be made public for the first time. He had tested some pipes into device, and as soon as it became dark he commenced lighting up. The device came out in a pale blue colour, but what was deficient in light was made up by a horrid smell, my father anxiously watching all the time, when all at once, a tremendous explosion was heard in the shop, the back windows of which were blown out, to the intense delight of the lookers-on, who thought that that was part of the performance, and applauded accordingly. However, my father saw that his experiment had not quite succeeded, and abandoned the idea of making gas.

N. NEABOM · FINISHED 1987

GREAT REJOICING

In 1820, the public spirit of the neighbourhood broke out in bells and candles. The occasion was the termination of the trial of *Queen Caroline, on the 10th of November; but in the absence of telegraphs and railways the news only reached here the next evening, when Beoley supplied the bells and Redditch the tallow, so that between the two a demonstration was made throughout the night, which might be considered by all parties a complete success.

Thursday, June 28th, 1838 was perhaps the gayest day ever seen in Redditch. It was the coronation of our much-loved Queen Victoria. All classes united in making it a glorious holiday. All the school children, headed by bands of music, paraded the town, and afterwards went to their several school rooms where they were regaled with roast beef and plum pudding. Two oxen, also, were roasted on the green, and about 600 persons were comfortably feasted. The afternoon and evening were spent in rural sports, and at midnight a grand display of fireworks finished off the day. All classes and sects thoroughly enjoyed the occasion; the leading manufacturers might be seen supplying the wants of the guests at the different tables, and some of the oldest men with the badge of Redditch - the white apron - on, carving away with all their might at the various dishes provided for "all comers", and strangest of all, the vicar and the Wesleyan minister went arm-in-arm amongst the people, as though they were servants of the same Master, and believed that the injunction in the New Testament to "Love one another" was really intended to be acted upon!

AMUSEMENTS

The amusements of Redditch were in some respects such as would become an Auburnian retreat, though frequently they were of a "rough and tumble" character. Until November 30th, 1821, a large horse chestnut tree stood on a high bank near the "big pool", where we met on summer evenings, and to the enlivening whistle of lame Ben Mitchell danced the happy hours away. There was also a sycamore tree on the Common, where we met and amused ourselves in the same manner. Here we met and had our recreation without the intervention of the public house, though of course there were many who squandered their money and wrecked their health in drunkenness, which was not necessary for their amusement. In old Redditch there were but few who took the trouble to cater for the amusement of the people, and consequently much rough and brutal sport was sought and followed.

**Queen Caroline was the divorced wife of George IV, she resided in Italy but returned to England in 1820 to defend her honour when a bill was brought in to dissolve her marriage on the grounds of her adultery.*

BULL-BAITING

One of the principal amusements was bull baiting, which took place in various parts of Redditch and neighbourhood. In the town, the favourite localities were behind old Ben Carr's house (where Mr Turner's steam mill now is), and at the back of the Tanhouse, where my father has often pointed out to me the post and the ring to which the bull was fastened. In a meadow near the Star and Garter, Crabbs Cross, there is yet to be seen such another post and ring; and here George Wells were "berrod" and looked to the interest of the bull, and saw fair play. The bull was fastened to the ring by a cord several yards long, and then the dogs were loosed at him. The true bull-dog made straight for his nose, and if he caught in any other place would keep changing his grip till he got hold of the desired point: but other dogs would rush at the nearest part, tail or nose being a matter of indifference to them. Often times the dog would be sent by the bull whirling in the air, and then all hands would run to the rescue and catch him ere he fell. Sometimes the bull would inflict great injuries on the dogs, in fact, it was an unusual thing to see a good dog with all his bones in their normal condition. One of the best dogs was Jem Wright's "Kit", but there were many favourites. The bull would generally be baited all day, and when he was tired, the "berrod" would throw a bucket of water over him to refresh him. At the end, the best appreciated part comes in, the "Smut". This was when all the dogs were set on the poor bull at one time. Occasionally, at this time, the bull was "accidentally" let loose, and then a general stampede finished up the sport.

COCK FIGHTING

Another favourite amusement of the neighbourhood was cock fighting. The most celebrated cock-pit was one kept by Joseph Lewis, at Crabbs Cross. It was made of gorse kids, with the sods turned up for the ring. People came from all parts to see the "mains" fought in this pit, and as many as five hundred persons at a time would pay their penny entrance to witness the "sport". There were three ways of fighting: the "long main" which generally continued for a week; the "short main", which was finished in a day or two; and the "battle royal", in which all the cocks were down at once, and the last cock left was the victor.

BAREFIST BOXING

The Redditch men for many years enjoyed (?) a reputation for fighting, and certainly if a readiness for battle showed a love for it, they must have had a continual feast in this line, for when there were no strangers to fight, friends had a few rounds, just to knock the "blue mould" off each other.

Several of the hardest fights of the Redditch men took place at Tanworth, the most noteworthy being between Perks and Bint, on the 18th May, 1929, and later a tremendous battle between Dick Stevens and J. Millington, January 22nd. Sometimes the people, in anticipation of a "big mill", would collect a purse and get two men to fight for it, as was the case at Headless Cross, when Tom Cook and Millington fought. Among the principal fighting men were the three brothers Archer, of Alcester, J. Heath and Batten, of Beoley. This Batten was employed as keeper under the Earl of Plymouth on account of his "plucky" character. He went on all right till one night he got too much of the old ale at the Hall, and set about the footman upon whom he left his mark in so many places that he had to leave his situation.

But of all the boxers, Smith, who kept the Plough, at Tanworth, was considered the king. He often came over to the Fox and Goose, got the pointers together, treated them well, and then induced them to fight him. He was a big man with extraordinary strength of limbs, and it was frightful to see and hear him hit when he warmed into his work.

One day he went to Hall Green races, and was staring at Chappell's show, when the showman suggested that if Smith would keep his mouth open he (Chappell) would like the privilege of jumping down his throat. Some "chaffing" went on and Smith offered to fight one of the troupe for £20 and young Chappell was fixed upon to give him a good drubbing. But he did not know his man, for though he was a wonderful fighter and gave Smith a good dressing down, he was obliged at last to strike his colours and bite the dust.

Smith had another great fight, beating Dunn, at Tanworth, on the 11th July 1825. Fights used to take place chiefly in the Pound Meadow, on the Green, at Crabbs Cross, Mappleborough Green, at the Old White Hart, Headless Cross, and later in the Bushy Piece.

RIVALRY AMONG POINTERS

The most terrible fighting I ever witnessed was at the White Hart, between a lot of pointers, who having met there to spend a quiet day, found the time hanging rather heavily on their hands, and so, by way of variant, turned out for a fight. They paired themselves according to weight and made the arrangement that no one should be permitted to fight more than three rounds, but these might be as long as they could make them. Knowing, therefore, how little time they had to "do business in" you may imagine the manner in which they set to work and execution they did.

Later I saw something of the same kind in Blind Lane, where while one pair were having their turn, the surrounding friends were making their arrangements "to keep the pot boiling"; and at the White Hart, once, during an offer of its kind, "Nail" Styler was so anxious to fight anybody that at last Dick Stevens consented to his wishes, knocked him on top of a wood-pile and would not let him come down again until he promised to "be good".

At the time when the canal was being made at the Tardebigge there was a good deal of fighting with the navvies, who were wont to come over in the evening, and amuse themselves after their day's toil with fighting the Redditch men in the Pound Meadow. But the most Donnybrook-like affair I ever saw was once at Foxlydiate Wake, when about forty navvies came over to engage the chivalry of Redditch. Everyone was obliged to fight or run. There were no "idle hands left to do the mischief" of a certain party often spoken of by Dr. Watts. From fists they came to sticks - it is said the navvies were provided with loaded ones. Palings were pulled up and a kid-pile being handy, all armed themselves and turned into Mr. Hemming's meadow and fought until the navvies "cut their sticks", after having had serious, if not fatal, injuries inflicted on two of their "butties".

But the times have changed, fighting has become unfashionable, and that which was once abundantly seen on every high hill and under every green tree has become of very rare occurrence. The other sports may be summed up as badger-baiting, dog-fighting, cock-throwing and etcetera. They were such as would make a rough and hardy population, and rough indeed we were. The "entertainment" shown to strangers was much the same in character as that shown by the inhabitant of the Black Country, who, when a person unknown in that locality was passing, suggested that his companion should "heave 'arf a brick at him".

MOUNTEBANKS

While treating of the amusements of Redditch, we may refer to the "Mountebanks". These men would take a field, and go through the ordinary routine of "rider" feats. No charge was made for admission, but during the performance tickets for a lottery were sold, and a number of things useful and ornamental were among the prizes gained. James Terry won the very useful prize of £5, May 28th, 1821.

PUBLIC CONCERTS

At this time the public concerts took place generally in the large room at the Crown, and were for the most part got up for special objects. For instance, one on the 20th December 1820, was for the benefit of David Clarkson and Samuel Richards. Another on the 6th of February 1822, was to buy David Clarkson a fiddle; and on February 18th 1824, for the benefit of Charles Scambler (a general favourite in Redditch) who had been unfortunate, and had got into difficulties. These were no "penny" entertainments, the tickets were 5s each, and the room generally was well-filled, many of the principal inhabitants acting as stewards.

STROLLING PLAYERS

The strolling players, too, were well supported in those days. Phillimore's used to perform in Wright's (now Brown's) band, on the Flat. Fenton's also played in the same place. On the 8th May, 1822, a company of players began to act in Keeper Horton's barn, opposite Mr. Holyoake's pin manufactury. On Saturday, May 15th, 1824, Potter & Company began to perform in a place specially put up by the builder, Gittens, and which is now part of Mr. Gregg's printing office. Later, the Rifle Corps Room became the playhouse of the town, and Jackman and his pretty daughters drew crowded houses. On the 17th of September, 1833, another amusement - that of horseracing - was added to the list. They were first held on Mr. Whadcoat's farm. This pastime, however, never took any particular hold of the Redditch people as a class, the majority of those present being strangers from Birmingham and elsewhere, with the usual mixture of card sharpers, garter prickers, and other swindlers.

HEMMING'S ENTRY

Most of the needle-making mills were spread along local rivers and streams. Redditch town centre did have some industrial sites but these were concentrated into small areas. Hemming's Entry still exists in parts. It began on Prospect Hill, went along Church Road and curved to go under the dual carriageway, came out in Melen Street, then branched off to go into Clive Road.

**After the needles had been put on the scouring bed for ten hours they were rinsed. The water that came off at this first washing was known as 'datment'.*

SHAVING HORSES' TAILS

Practical joking was very prevalent, and it succeeded very well with the Redditch lads, as they were equally ready to laugh or fight at the result. Shaving horses' tails and cutting harness were among some of the most heartless and senseless of their "larks". Sometimes when a pedlar came to one of the mills, a party would engage his attention at one of the lower beds while another from above would pour a bucket of *"datment" over the poor fellow and his "cast-iron" knives, and when Autolycus expressed his disapproval of his proceeding they would drag him through the mill-pond, which would fix the

grease rather than remove it. But the viciousness of this kind of sport has passed away; civilisation and good sense have taken Redditch in their course, and the impulses of mind which led to these excesses being turned in other directions, have made its population among the sharpest and quickest-witted of men.

WHIPPING FOR THE MAN WHO LEFT HIS WIFE

Whipping in public had been much resorted to as a punishment for offences against the law, but was now becoming much less used, and on the 3rd of February, 1819, we went to Holt End, to see the last application of the cat-o'-nine-tails in this neighbourhood, when a man was flogged through the village for deserting his wife.

A PUBLIC HANGING

On the 22nd March, 1822, a party of us went on Humphries' coach to Worcester, to see Guest and Brettle hung for ill-treating Thomas Hood, a tailor, of Beoley; but great was our disappointment, for their lawyer got Hood, who could not read, to put his cross to a paper, which resulted in a reprieve for them and a "sell" for us. We should have been only too glad to see Hood and the lawyer hung out in the culprits' places. But hangings were everyday matters in those times, and I remember that out of less than 100 prisoners tried at the Lent Assizes in 1827, twenty-four of them were sentenced to death.

THE FOOT MESSENGER

The early postal arrangements of the town were exceeding simple and unassuming. Once a week a foot messenger came from Henley into the town, with a horn, which he blew to give notice of his arrival. He would then distribute his letters, and receive others "if any", as the old clerk Davis used to say of the children to be baptized. He would then go on his way and send them off at his convenience.

Afterwards the post office became more regular under the superintendence of Mr. Thomas Mence, down in Littleworth, till on the 24th September, 1828, it was removed to Dr. Taylor's, where, under the superintendence of Miss

Taylor, it so grew in efficiency and importance that one despatch daily became insufficient and two distributions were necessary. Perhaps no town of so small a size has so large and extended a correspondence. There is no town in the kingdom but exchanges letters with us, and every country in the civilized world (and some indeed in the uncivilized) are in constant communication with our town, which they know and address as "Reddech". "Reddith", Reddich", "Blunts, Worcestershire", "Sharps", "Betweens", "Ground Downs", and so on, all of which directions mean Redditch, and find their way here.

The year 1840 was one of great importance, not only to Redditch, but also to the country at large, as being the year in which the postage of letters was reduced to a penny. The post office resources must have been taxed to their very utmost, for I believe that almost every man who had a friend made an excuse to send a letter, and those who had not a friend sent an unpaid missive to an enemy, leaving him to pay the postage, which was double.

THE FORTUNE'S COMING

At this time took place one of the few romantic incidents occurring in Redditch, and which created considerable excitement amongst the inhabitants. A Mr. Lawrence had died in Virginia, and left a large sum of money, which was claimed, among others, by some families in Redditch. Of course much and long litigation was the consequence, till on the 27th June, 1829, Mr. Cresswell came down from London with 10,000 as a first instalment of the property, for the benefit of the local claimants. This, however, was but a small portion of the amount left by Lawrence, and the remaining part was supposed to have been kept in the hands of the lawyers to carry on the case with, for not a penny more ever found its way to Redditch. "Great expectations" kept the matter alive for a long time, and "the fortunes coming" became a proverb amongst us. One of the most amusing parts of the matter was the number of friends who sprang up in all directions round the expectants; one of whom, an old man at Headless Cross, had a hare given to him by a gentleman at Coughton. Charles had not had such a thing in his larder before, but in due course justice was done to it. Some time after Charles said to his wife, "I'm going to Coughton today and perhaps Mr Morgan will give me another hare". His wife instantly exclaimed, "For goodness sake don't ever bring another hare, for I had such work with the last that I thought I should never have done picking it."

THE TERROR OF CHOLERA

The year 1832 will be long remembered with dread as the year when the cholera raged with such frightful virulence throughout the country, and in few places in the kingdom was it more deadly than in Redditch. The first which fell a victim here was John Lead, and the second the wife of George Parsons, who lived opposite "The Woodland Cottage" at the end of The Flat. Then followed such a terrible succession of deaths, that some left the neighbourhood in terror. Cases occurred in which the men were well at night and buried next morning, and well can I remember the deep anxiety with which in the morning we enquired who had been the victims during the night. Owing to the dread of contagion, so quickly were the bodies buried that it was feared that in some cases sufficient precaution had not been taken, and that, at least in one instance, a person had been buried alive.

The 21st March was set apart as a day of humiliation and prayer, and later, a town's meeting was called, and some cottages in the Old Hop Gardens, near the Old Railway Station, were used as a kind of hospital for the sick. However, the people were not satisfied, and the town petitioned the Government for instructions how they were to act, and a reply was returned, advising the formation of a Local Board of Health. This was at once done, a dispensary was opened at Hall's, the grocer, and anyone, night or day, could obtain medicine free. Young Mr. Pratt, the surgeon, was in constant attendance here, and administered to the wants of the people. Throughout the summer the pestilence raged, and most families suffered from it; in some instances as many as three died. I have been looking over a private list which I jotted down at the time, and I find the names of fifty persons I know who succumbed to the pestilence.

It was not until the autumn that the disease abated, and the 14th December was appointed a day of heartfelt thanksgiving that this scourge had disappeared. During its existence there was great religious excitement. Special services were held in the chapels, and many of the most vicious characters of the town became changed men, and for years sustained the principal offices of their churches. I must here pay a tribute to the ministers of the town, who, seemingly careless of themselves, were ever ready to give help when needed, and at the bedside of the dying, and in the families of the dead, were to be found exercising their holy functions.

SMALLPOX

While on this subject I may allude to a later time - 1838 - when smallpox was extremely fatal. On the 23rd December, John Haden, a young man with a wooden leg, died. Quiney, of the Horse and Jockey, buried five children in three weeks; and William and Ann Webb, four in a fortnight; and Henry Humphries, three in about nine days.

REDDITCH CHARTISTS

With respect to political feeling, it never ran very high in Redditch, though previous to the *Chartist movement a branch of the Political Union was established at the Black Horse, kept by John Whateley, one of the principal movers in it being Mr.Whitehouse, of Hardwick. The members of this union were amongst the first to help Feargus O'Connor in his effort to gain "the five points of the Charter". A meeting - the first of the kind in the town - was held at the Warwick Arms, some time in 1832, presided over by Mr. Whitehouse. On the 15th July, 1839, Bourne's house, as well as others, in Birmingham were burnt, and this warmed up the Redditch Chartists. On the 13th January 1841, they commenced to hold their meetings at the Round House, then the property of Mr. Whitehouse. Afterwards, a "Chartist Hall" was built on the premises of Thos Prescott, at the bottom of the Back Hill. It was raised by an unlimited liability company, shares, 5s. each. In this building some of the most prominent Chartist lecturers held forth, including George White, Dr. McDonald, and others. Feargus O'Connor was engaged to come, but failed to put in an appearance.

After the building was not required for political purposes the shares fell through, and then, like Goldies' chest of drawers, it a "double debt contrived to pay", and Alexander-like, when its glory had departed, became a thing of usefulness, and the weary tramp and artful dodger made it their rallying point, and beds and lodgers were crammed into every corner, so that it became itself at last a place of universal "suffer-age".

There were but few who became very excited over the Charter, with the exception of one who shall be nameless. He said his horse should have nothing to eat till the Charter was gained. This was no very great change for the animal, which went on pretty well for a time; but at length it died with the Charter, somehow or other. Perhaps both were ridden to death.

**The Chartist movement was a national one, demanding a number of political reforms. It was at its height in the late 1930's and lasted for about 20 years. At one time it was led by Feargus O'Connor.*

SANITARY ARRANGEMENTS IMPROVED

One of the first steps towards the sanitary improvement of the town was commenced on the 10th April, 1843, when the pool opposite the house of Mr. A G. Baylis was let dry. This pond was doubtless of great antiquity and had, in its brighter days, served to feed the moat which formerly surrounded the half-timbered buildings now known as *Salter's Yard, but which must have been when the moat was in existence, a sort of manor house, or better kind of farmhouse. However, at this time, 1843, its character may be judged from the many aliases it had - "Tanner's Pool", "Sheward's Pool", "Big Pool", etcetera, etcetera. It was filled with stagnant water, dotted over pretty freely with the mortal remains of murdered dogs and slaughtered cats. It seemed to be the receptacle of all the refuse of the town, and a walk along its banks on a warm day was sufficient to satisfy the appetite for the next six hours. Had the place existed in its old form until the present day, it must, with our increased population, have kept plague and fever ever in our midst. In the olden times the pool was open to the road at the end, and I can remember that William Turner's wife was drowned in it January 1st, 1829, and Thomas Nash met with the same fate on the 10th February, 1837.

LIGHTNING AND LIGHTING IN 1843

On the 9th August, 1843, the town was visited by an awful thunderstorm. Terrible consternation prevailed, many believing that the last day had come. For hours, the tempest hung about the town, the lightning being unusually vivid and the thunder tremendous, while the rain came down like a deluge, filling cellars and flooding everywhere. One very remarkable thing was noticed, that all the places of worship were more or less uninjured by the lightning, but no serious damage was done anywhere, except by the water.

During the year 1843, Mr. Thomas Mees came into the town and commenced preparations for supplying the town with gas. Redditch had once before - as long ago as November, 1831 - been lit up with oil lamps, at a time when the town was infested with a gang of robbers who carried on their depredations so skilfully that although robberies were of daily occurrence, none of the culprits could be detected. We used to laugh at the suggestion that there was a need for our constables to be vaccinated, because, we told them, they "never caught anything". Well, the streets were lit with lamps, special constables were appointed; six of whom, under the direction of Police-

**Salter's Square, which we assume to be Salter's Yard, lay between Queen Street and Grove Street, opposite the Council House, near or on the site of the Palace Theatre.*

Constable Freeth, who was brought over for the purpose, paraded the streets every night. As the robberies diminished, so the lamps went out, and through the long nights darkness reigned again.

However, on the 13th December, 1843, gas was used for the first time in the streets, and on the 24th December, 1844, the town was lit up. This was a private arrangement which soon fell through, and the streets remained in the ancient dreariness, and it was not until the Local Board took the matter up that anything of a permanent nature was done to illuminate the town.

LOADING THE COACH

COACHING DAYS

It may interest some who take the trouble to read these records to have some idea of the early coaches of the county. On October 21st, 1808, a new double-bodied post coach was advertised to run from Worcester to London three days a week, starting from Worcester at noon, and arriving in London at eight the next morning. On May 1st 1833, the "Hirondelle" coach, which passed through Worcester, was driven from Liverpool to Worcester, a distance of 136 miles, in nine hours and thirty-three minutes. Fourteen miles an hour including stoppages.

The question has been asked, how did we get out of Redditch to Birmingham and back? Well, the first means of public conveyance to Birmingham was by Clarkes' "Needle" Coach, which was made more for use than ornament. It was also known as the "lagabooby" and passengers going by it had to meet it at the Portway. Afterwards Heath commenced to run a coach direct from Redditch, and was succeeded by Edward Humphreys. On the 30th September, 1824, Richard Humphreys commenced running his coach, but sold it in May, 1829, to Mr. Ashwin. He soon, however, altered his mind, and began again, and for many years was the principal medium of communication between Redditch and the world in general. The coach ran through Beoley, and though pretty punctual in starting, its arrival in Redditch was not sufficiently accurate to regulate one's clock by. All that was required was that it should be back in time to start again next morning. The *piece de resistance* was an excellent inn, called the Cross and Bowling Green, where, on coming back, it has been said, the passengers would alight and play at cards for legs of mutton and trimmings; and one night they were so long about it that it was said (perhaps by some railway shareholder) that the sheep had to be caught and killed after its leg had been lost and won. After this, Roberts, Terrill and Stanley, increased the accommodation, and it was quite amusing to see the spirit of rivalry with respect to bringing into the town the largest load. I well remember coming in one night with the old veteran, and a gentleman who lived midway up Fish Hill asked to get down at the bottom. But Richard did not want to lose one of his show, and said to his passenger, "Now please do oblige me this once, and ride up into the town." Another straw would, however, have broken the horses' backs.

THE LONDON WAGGON

Redditch was becoming such a place of importance, that in the early part of May, 1821, the first regular public conveyance commenced its journey through the town. This was the "London Waggon", which was started by the firm of Berry & Harris, glass manufacturers, to carry their goods to London, picking up what they could on the road. It was an extraordinary machine, the wheels having each six rows of three-inch tyres, and were so wide that they were called the "London rollers", and so useful were they to the roads that only a small toll was charged in consequence. When it was in progress it was drawn by from seven to twelve horses, and was more like the progress of an Eastern dignitary than the conveyance of Midland goods to London. The waggon left Stourbridge early on Sunday morning, and we had to meet it with our goods at the Unicorn about tea time. It then proceeded along the upper road by way of Alcester, Shipston and Oxford etcetera, to London, arriving at the Castle and Falcon, Aldersgate Street, "weather permitting", on Wednesday night. The charge for heavy goods was 12s 6d per cwt. Berry and Harris sold their carrying trade to Rufford, who afterwards transferred it to Jolly & Sons.

THE TARDEBIGGE CANAL

I may mention here that on the 4th December, 1815, the Worcester and Birmingham Canal was opened. From the Severn to Tardebigge, fifteen miles, there is a rise of 428 feet, with 74 locks. From Tardebigge to Birmingham, 14 miles, it is level. At Westheath there is a tunnel 2,700 yards in length.

THE COMING OF THE RAILWAYS

We were now getting connected in a measure with railways, for on the 27th May, 1844, an omnibus commenced running to Barnt Green in connection with the railway. By the way, it seemed to be part of the plan of the Midland Railway directors to make their line so that no place should be much accommodated by it, so we were left five miles distant; and it also seemed curious that although in the year 1845 there were twenty-seven schemes of railways advertised for the county of Worcester, not one of the whole number was to include Redditch.

ON REFLECTION

I now bring what I have to say to a conclusion. I have been absent from the town for many years, but my heart is still with the home of my youth. I often thought that a history of Redditch might be useful and interesting, and looking over my father's papers - poor man, he fell a victim to cholera in 1832 - I found that he had projected a history of Redditch, which of course he never carried out; but his memoranda may perhaps be useful to a future historian, and I have therefore arranged and added to them as best I could, and if others who read this will add what they know, in a short time a full history of Redditch might be written.

REDDITCH AND THE NEEDLES AFTER WILLIAM AVERY
A personal view by Norman Neasom

Norman Neasom comes from an old Redditch family, his grandfather lived in the Red House (next to the old Smallwood Hospital) and was well known in the town as a founder member of Neasom and White, the Auctioneers and Surveyors.

Norman was born in a cottage in Brockhill Lane in 1915 and at sixteen, he went to Birmingham College of Art. On leaving he helped with the family farms at Birchensale and Lowanshill but spent his evenings and every spare moment sketching and painting. When world war II ended the Birmingham College of Art had its first large intake and Norman was asked to return as tutor. He also taught at Bournville and Aston.

In 1953 he was offered a post at the Redditch School of Art, eventually becoming head of the art department. He retired a year early to pursue his creative talents, having become a member of the Royal Birmingham Society of Artists and the prestigious Royal Water Colour Society

Old Redditch was a fine country town. St Stephen's church was in the centre on the old village green, and the surrounding Georgian houses gave Redditch a spacious elegance. The town was situated at the northern end of a prehistoric ridgeway so that you could see green hills in whichever direction you looked.

The people seemed quite different in Redditch to any other town. Perhaps it was because many of them were involved in the same industry. Their dialect was unique, said to be evolved from shouting over the stamping presses! If you went into Redditch you could guarantee that you would know half the people you passed in the street. The locals were always friendly and ready to help, and they had an enthusiasm for life which I have not found elsewhere. The annual carnival, for example, was reckoned to be the best in the Midlands and people came from all the surrounding counties to see it.

During the great depression of the 1920's, which I remember, there was never a lot of unemployment in Redditch. Although the large employers such as Terry's, Royal Enfield and BSA did not pay high wages, they managed to keep their firms going. In other parts of the country, a large proportion of the population were out of work

My parents were busy farmers and so they always had a maid. Lilian Field was one who stayed with us for many years. When she had finished her work, usually in the evenings, she would set up her little industrial vice in the kitchen. There she would sit with her large box of feathers, cottons, twills and silks, tying flies onto the fish hooks. She was as quick as lightning and fascinating to watch.

There was an enormous amount of this kind of activity in the town. Almost everyone in Redditch was involved in one way or another in needles - or fishing hooks or springs, both obvious developments from the needle trade. There was also a lot of rod-making, another natural development, together with various metal-based products. Even the Royal Enfield motor cycles came about through a needle-manufacturer diversifying into bicycle-making.

It was a sad day when, in 1963, Sir Keith Joseph, Minister of Housing and Local Government, announced that Redditch was to be designated as a New Town. Now the green valleys have become housing estates, the town is full of strangers and the heart of the town, the Kingfisher Shopping Centre, belongs not to the Redditch Borough Council but to financiers in London!

As for the needle industry, very little now remains. The oldest is Richard Allen Medical Industries (UK) Ltd, which still uses some of the original buildings and equipment, and has a couple of dozen workers making surgical needles. There are a few companies with about fifty personnel, among them Surgicraft

Ltd (surgical needles), Foster Needle Ltd (felting needles to go into looms) and William Smith & Son (Neptune Works) Ltd, (sailmaker's needles). Maersk Medical Ltd employs 140 in Redditch and 300 in the UK in the manufacture of non-active medical devices, of which needles are a small part.

The Needle Industries at Studley was once the largest manufacturer of needles in the world and, at its peak between 1950 and 1970, it employed about fifteen hundred people. Saved only by a management buy-out in 1991, it has now been renamed Entaco Ltd and has about two hundred employees producing approximately ten million hand-sewing needles each week.

I only have to walk a short way from my house before I can see the roofs of the Kingfisher Shopping Centre, and when I catch sight of them I feel a great nostalgia, and a sadness that this happy little town has changed beyond recognition and its great needle industry is no more.

APPENDIX - FORGE MILL

The following were the processes used in needle-making when Forge Mill was at its height:

Steel wire was drawn through a series of tiny holes to achieve the correct thickness and cut into pieces the length of two needles. Needles were (and still are) made two at a time. The wire was straightened to remove any curvature. Points were made by holding each end of the wire in turn against a grindstone. The kick stamp made the indentations for the eyes and the Fly Press punched the holes.

The needles were threaded on to thin strips of metal called 'spits', put in a clamp to remove any excess metal and the two needles were broken into single needles.

Forge Mill is one of Redditch's old needle scouring mills. It was built as an iron forge early in the eighteenth century but converted to needle scouring in about 1730. Over two hundred years later it was still operating commercially. After its closure in 1958 it was acquired by the Redditch District Council and converted into an Industrial Museum.

They were heated to 800 degrees centigrade to harden them, then to 200 degrees to make them less brittle.They were now ready to be sent to Forge Mill for scouring. Needles were layered with abrasives, wrapped in canvas and hessian and placed under the scouring runners for anything from one day to a week, depending on the type of needle. The abrasives were checked and replaced at regular intervals.

The needles were given a final polish under the scouring runners with a layer of putty powder and olive oil, then dried in revolving barrels full of sawdust. From here they were put into Fanning Out trays to separate the needles from the sawdust, on the winnowing principle. They were then ready to be packed in brown paper and returned to the original manufacturer who would inspect, pack into tiny needle packets and despatch.

(Taken from the guide to Forge Mill Museum where these processes are described in detail)

ERRATUM

Acknowledgements
'Who was then living' ie in 1887, when the booklet was first published.

Redditch and the Needles before William Avery
Further excavations have now been carried out at Bordesley Abbey and no evidence of needle-making has been found. Earliest references to needle-making in the area are to a William Lea (from London) in Studley during the second quarter of the 17th century.

Page 30 BAREFIST BOXING (sixth line) took place on 18th May 1829 not 1929.

Page 37 REDDITCH CHARTISTS (note in margin). The movement was at its height in the late 1830's and not 1930's